my
PERCEPTION
DECEIVED ME

TANESHA RIVERS

CONTENTS

CHAPTER 1

I went from being an evangelist to a pastor months after I wrote The Strength and Struggle of a Woman. This is a continuation of that book. I was in and out of the states like I was selling something. I was having the time of my life and enjoying myself. My babies were safe and I was partying like a rockstar. My trip to Tulum, Mexico was the best one that I have been on thus far. I was in airports frequently; it was a dream come true for me. All I desired to do was smile and travel. I met some amazing people while on vacation, to the point where I was like, Hey, I am divorced, happy, and healthy, and it feels wonderful to be free.

Of course, I was still evangelizing and doing my prayer daily with women across the world. I was dating different types of people. None of them seemed to get my attention. Either their brains were empty or everything turned me off. The dates were beautiful and I was enjoying the dating life. Dates were literally $400.00 every time I went out. I painted my own canvas, and because I was single, I was doing what I wanted to do. Having no attachments, no obligations, and no one knowing where I lived was awesome. Every guy seemed to take interest in me quickly, and for some strange reason, I was turned off. No one was saved and no one was my type. After all, did I have a type? The more and more people called me, the more annoyed I became. There was always someone interested in me and I was living my best life. Either people lacked motivation, or they presented an idea that they thought would interest me, but it didn't. Either dudes had little knowledge or we just weren't into the same things. I was dating, but my ultimate goal was to please God. You can date, sis! Whew, chile, it was fun, but annoying.

I received flowers and expensive dates. Growing up as a Jersey girl, dates are mandatory. We love someone to romance us ladies. We get dressed and show up with class on our dates. The men pay and we leave the tips. I was leaving tips after all these expensive dates; that's the least I could do. It's 2022 and guys don't want to pay for everything. I totally understand. He needs to know that you can hold your own as well. Pay attention, sis! These dudes were coming harder and harder each day.

CHAPTER 2

I was living and, baby, I was enjoying myself. My friend, Rick, had just come home from prison, and it was great. We became workout partners and we were challenging ourselves to be better. He never switched up on me, and that made me feel safe. Everything was different for him. His mother was now deceased. I had to walk him through stuff that his mother normally did for him. It was a little scary, but he conquered and became independent quickly. I was so proud of him as he came home and got himself a job seven days after his release from prison. He was moving fast, and it was outstanding for him to beat the odds so quickly. He was eager to transform his mind, and I was eager to help him through his transformation. He was Muslim and I am Christian, but he was my person, and for me, it was his soul that mattered most. Lo and behold, he was my hangout partner, and it was cool. Madison loved seeing him come around. She loved to be around him. It was super adorable. It felt good to see him around. We went into the community together to help him readjust to society. Society was different for him; people being too close to him made him want to fight anybody. It's funny now, but it was difficult to watch him experience this. In the beginning, it was so hard for him to adjust to people.

I encouraged Rick and told him I believed in him. He is the best rapper ever, and I spoke life into him daily. He was working, rapping, doing photoshoots, and feeling himself. I was his personal hype man. I was all in, and he was taking off quickly. Rappers were reaching out to him and he believed that he could achieve his dreams. His self-esteem was rising, and so was his following.

Lo and behold, he has, and will always have, a special place in my heart. He was the one who was always solid. You have to respect those who never switch up on you. His brother and I had ups and downs, but he remained neutral. I put my ideas in the closet just to get him together. My ideas were important, but I always try to assist when I can, especially those who have always shown me love... I hope you are not bored because baby, my perception deceived me.

I was working out hard and trying to get in shape for the summer. Good things were happening for me and I was excited. My passion has always been serving God's people. I just have to be careful because serving too much steals my time—the time I can spend producing something, creating something, making something of myself. I was his taxi driver because his driver's license was suspended. I made appointments for him. I stepped up when I could, but still, I have my own life.

My ministry is so important to me. My love and loyalty get me in trouble every time. When you try to do good, things always come back to haunt you. I did a lot of things in my life, and now, I live in regret because my heart is sincere for people. I was carrying a lot. Slowly but surely, however, I was discarding things that were not beneficial to my mental health. Mentally, I was carrying a lot and still trying to look out for people. That slapped me dead in the face. It was crazy, but it was life.

CHAPTER 3

I met this one dude, and he had my attention after six months spent away from social media. His face was the first one I saw on my list of friend requests. He wasn't my cup of tea, but he was what I needed. He came on my prayer line and said God was going to send me a husband. I was listening to him, but the ultimate goal was to knock every goal out of the park. We started conversing a lot after I gave him an invitation to be a guest on my prayer line. I paid him like I always do, because he walked heavily and he did an outstanding job. Walking heavily meant he was speaking life to everyone who was on the line, and he was very accurate. He asked when I would have him back on the line. I told him soon. He would fill in for me when I didn't have the strength to do it on my own. There's nothing like a praying man. Right, sis?

My mother was not excited at the beginning of our friendship. We formed a relationship that was healthy. My mom told me he would not be my husband. I didn't care what others had to say concerning what I felt. I don't care what others have to say about my decisions. I always live my life that way. Good or bad, someone is always going to have something to say. At the end of the day, I'm going to do what I feel is best for me at any cost. At this time, I was a financial advisor. I was extremely busy trying to get my life in order and help others at the same time. I am in my late thirties, and I am growing as an entrepreneur and a leader.

My biological brother, Marco, was so excited for my new relationship. He told me that my new partner reminded him of my first love. I don't know why Marco told me that. I loved that man with my whole heart. That was the best feeling ever. My brother and I are extremely close. Our bond is unbreakable. Nothing can separate us from one another.

I had staff in my home daily. Every day, someone relieved me of the cares of life. I had a personal cook, cleaner, errand runner, and other people to help with my life. I had it made. My staff were so happy that my countenance changed. They were also excited because my boo made me smile and laugh. He was protecting me and praying for me, and I was relieved from the agony. The pain lifted immediately; I stopped feeling pain. The only emotions I felt were happiness and joy. He was consistent and great with words, and those qualities were so attractive. He was so intelligent. I will take intelligence over anything, any day. Mind over matter.

I started calling him my prince. "Prince" was befitting for him with the things he was doing for me in a short period of time—nothing financial, but spiritually, he was fighting for me. My prince spoke life into me freely, and his affirmations were accurate. Every day, I received paragraphs with correct spelling and punctuation. Whew, chile, he can read, write, and spell, I thought. This was outstanding to witness.

I am too old to be dealing with drug dealers and dodo birds. Prince said that I should get a website and rebrand myself. He informed me that he purchased the highest package for his website, and suggested that I do the same. I was beyond cheesy; he really cared about my presentation and the way I looked. We scheduled a meeting with the owner, and Prince was on the call as well. Prince was there to support me. The CEO asked me numerous questions, and I answered them to the best of my ability because I didn't understand the coded language he was speaking. I don't like technology, but I can do a few things. I am more of a reader—a little bookworm. I love old-school reading and researching.

I gained a liking for the CEO of the company, John; his personality was unmatched. His spirit was similar to mine. He just wanted to see me win, and I loved the idea. He was calling me "iconic" and "mega." Although people may see me as that, they refrain from telling me. Honestly, I appreciated, and still appreciate, his kind words and gestures. No matter what I do or where I go, I have to remain meek and humble. John and I talked daily, just as much as Prince and I did. Prince started calling John and I "best friends." I was in agreement with him calling us BFFs because he had so much potential, like me.

We had so many things in common. He was super smart, and I enjoyed listening to him and bouncing my ideas off of him. Some days, he would do things for me for free out of the kindness of his heart. He sent me some earrings in the mail. He was always looking out for me, and that was a bonus. You find people who seemingly look out for you, but have hidden motives. Nothing in life was free, and I was tired of doing things for people at no charge.

I was still traveling and talking to my new best friend. Prince and John were best friends as well. Our best friend was my boo. I started calling him my boo. Prince was royalty to me, and he carried himself in that manner. He was royalty at its best, and I wanted to treat him as such. I am a queen, and I am delighted to get what I deserve. I really have been through some heavy trials, but I still have my right mind. I did not let anything make me bitter or stagnant. I talked to both of them on Facebook Messenger every day. We called each other daily. Prince knew my schedule, and I knew his. We communicated daily, and I enjoyed the fact that while Prince wasn't a big talker, he expressed himself when he needed to. He could walk into rooms with me and not embarrass me because he was diverse. He was a white man, and he took pride in being white. He was using me on his platform, and I was doing the same. We were the perfect duo. He made statements to help advance me, and I loved that. When someone wants you to win, they help you win. I am a strong believer of that.

How could two walk together unless they agree? They agree to work together, agree to stand together, agree to band together, agree to work on themselves, agree to disagree. My goal, my motive, was always to please God. I am a woman who lives a consecrated life so that I can hear from heaven. I told Prince that fasting and prayer is my life. He said I didn't have to do all of that with him walking alongside me. I felt relieved because I didn't have to be so deep anymore. That was wonderful. Pay attention. I sure wish that I did!

CHAPTER 4

Whew, chile. Your head is about to spin.

I had never met Prince in person, and I was driving to Georgia for his birthday. This was nerve-racking for me because I didn't know what to expect. I had all these ideas in my mind: What if he doesn't like me in person? What if he thinks I don't look the same as I do online? The devil was playing tricks on my mind.

I was driving because it was his birthday and I wanted to make it elegant and classy. I needed to bring my balloon machine, beautiful plates, and menus. I wanted to show him how a prince is supposed to be treated. I was digging him from the beginning, through the middle, and all the way to the end.

I made sure I brought my A-game so he could feel appreciated. I wanted everything to be solely about me and him. I presented him with roses, candles, and rose petals. I had never given a man roses before. I purchased cake and all the fancy things. It was so special to me. When we first saw one another, we were wearing the same color—all black. It was like magic, and I was ready to pull something out of my hat. The prince was tall and had long legs. We drove around Georgia and chilled together. I was excited that we were getting along in person. He purchased me some AirPods and threw my bootleg ones out the window. It made me excited that he was thinking about my presentation.

We spent some days together and I didn't want to return to New Jersey. His personality was laid-back and reserved, for the most part. I was used to foolishness, and I began to bask in how calm he was. We were cuddling, watching Animal Planet. We both wanted pet monkeys and I thought that was cool—two weirdos who could live in each other's worlds. I know that I am very peculiar, and when I meet someone who's like me, I am happy. Sometimes, it appears that I am living in a box and no one can relate to me. The most prophetic being lives in this world, and I do my best to try to stay under the radar. We went out for some food and enjoyed ourselves.

Prince appeared to be bossy. He bossed around my respite worker, who had come to visit our best friend. I tried to hook them up, but that didn't work out well. We had the nicest Airbnb, which had a lot of potential. I went for my daily walks while I was there.

After months of being on the phone, he was cool as ever in person. I could see us being together forever. With us being two like-minded folks, what could go wrong?

CHAPTER 5

Prince was having a party in Georgia and wanted to invite his family. One month after first seeing him, we were about to meet again. Prince and I talked about ministry and life. We talked about family and were in agreement about everything.

Prince wanted me and my family to come to Georgia on August 9, 2021. I was happy to finally meet his mom. He would have me reach out to her and chat with her periodically. He wanted his family to love and accept me. I am cool, witty, crazy, bold, and myself, so why wouldn't they? It was a party, and I wanted to get my makeup together and get dolled up. I didn't get to the event until 9 p.m. He wanted me to wear my red bottoms and come looking sexy. I was always excited about dressing up.

I changed clothes and went to the hall where everyone was waiting. I saw our best friend, John, and I was so happy. I gave him a hug and was so happy to just see his face. Prince got to meet Madison in person. He always video chatted with me and saw her as well. We played games together. We laughed and joked. I got to meet his brother, who was a nurse, and I was excited because Prince looked up to him. His name was Jayden. We talked, and Jayden said that I had made Prince bougie. Prince was dressed nicely and looked very clean. I had already fallen in love, and I let him know how I was feeling daily.

Things were moving fast, but hey, we'd both been married before. People know what they want in life. He told me that he felt the same way about me. Whew, chile, he made my heart melt. I was on cloud nine. Prince cooked for the event, and the food was great. My mom flew in with us. She said his food needed salt. I didn't care what it needed—my prince cooked. He decorated as well, and his decoration skills were impressive for a man. I decorate, too, so I was impressed that he had done all of this by himself. John said it would be epic. He had a blow-up projector. It was thoughtful and nice. We were playing bingo, and I won one game. I won $75.00 and kept saying it was my birthday.

He wanted his family to like me so badly. That was a fear of his. I always told him they would, and that I would always be myself. Prince lived with his best friend, Sarah, at this time. I wanted to know how she became his best friend so fast. He told me to ask myself how he got me so fast. We laughed. He had not been in Georgia for a long time. His facial expression was always serious. He had a "don't play with me" look. He was so young, but he had no kids, no drama, no messy things going on. I actually got to meet his best friend, Sarah. She was looking at me strangely as I walked into the room. I know that look as a woman. I am observant of all things around me. It appeared as if she wanted to tell me something. She told me she would tell me exactly who she was. I was okay with that. I didn't feel any insecurity about her.

A lot of women are attracted to him because he is anointed. That was not the case for me; I didn't pay that any mind. He captured my attention with his words; his words were fresh wind blowing through my hair. It was the look in his eyes for me. I am an eye person. The eyes tell a lot about a person. Sarah was also our BFF's auntie;

his family filled the room. It was very intimate. I left my son with our family because at this time, he was misbehaving. Whew, chile, he was robbing people at the age of twelve. Mentally, I was exhausted from my son.

We always gave our son whatever he wanted. My ex-husband, JW, and I spoil our children. People who normally rob others are lacking things. That was my perception at that time. He had everything, including an iPhone. His birthday was approaching and I planned a trip to Disney World. I love to show my babies how special they are, and birthdays are everything to me. My son came home one day and was looking suspicious. I asked him what he had just done, and he said nothing. He went back and forth to the window, looking as if he was waiting for someone to appear. My gifts began to work. I said, "You just did something wrong." Soon after he went to shower, someone began banging on the door. The police were at my door. They were asking me to come downstairs so they could speak to me. I went down, and they explained that my son fit the description of a robber. I asked, "Why would my son take something that he already has?" I knew there was some truth to the story because he was walking back and forth like something was wrong. You know how people pace when something is bothering them.

I told the police to let me go talk to him. I did just that, and he invited the police to check him and his room because he didn't do anything. I was on my baby's side, but I knew something was off at that moment. Us mothers ride with our children. They searched his room and found nothing. They took his clothes for evidence and looked everywhere. My son kept lying, saying he didn't have the phone. The cops searched diligently because Bergen County police don't get much action. The crime rate is extremely low in this area. There were ten police cars outside of my house as if my son was an adult. The police called the phone and located the device in my next-door neighbor's backyard.

It was so disheartening to hear that my son had pushed a fifty-plus-year-old lady down to the floor to snatch her iPhone out of her hand. But honey, chile, he did it and had no remorse. His facial expression communicated, "Oh, well." I asked him why he would do something like this. He stated that his iPhone broke, and he thought I was going to be mad because I had just fixed his phone. I said, "I'm upset because you snatched someone else's phone. You were just about to get the latest phone on your birthday, son." Talk about perception, baby.

I was looking at this child crazy because he was the golden child. The one who got everything that he wanted. The one who did his chores, washed clothes, washed dishes, and shoveled snow for our neighbors. I was appalled! Prince was on the phone with me, and I was in disbelief. My baby had gone wild. I was doing ministry and positive things, and my baby was up to no good.

That's normally how ministry works. A thorn had to be in my flesh. I was mentally tired from everything: the drama, my staff, their laziness—or, should I say, their level of comfort. My mom was driving me crazy. Everything around me was going up in flames. Prince was there interceding for me and telling me he had to get me out of that environment. I agreed that it was toxic, and the more I tried to move forward, here came a problem and an issue. Lord knows I was tired and aggravated with everyone around me. It was hard to see each one's motives because they all were saying, "I love you, T. I am here for you, T." Everyone had the same language and the same faces. I had Sally, one of my workers, in my presence trying to take advantage of me. I had my family always pulling me in every direction.

If something happened to me, people were going to be lost. I had my ministry that I was trying to hold together. Life was still happening. I had my in-laws who I was attached to, and it was hard to let go of them. It was hard to disown people who I had built a relationship with for years. Although people did things to me, I did things that were toxic as well. I can always own my stuff. I love from the core of my belly. These were people whose children I had raised and built up. These were people I vacationed with and had memories and pictures with. I was over here in my own thoughts, saying to myself, Let it go. It's been this way for so long, and it's still not working for you. Why do you want to partake in environments that were set up to destroy you? When you turn your back, they are talking about you. When you help people, it's taken out of context, anyway. I was torn between old and new. My prince was there, pouring into me and pulling on me to escape this world. "God has more for you," said Prince.

People are your worst force!

CHAPTER 6

Keep reading!

The people who you love could kill you.

I was relieved for my ex-husband to take our son after this pandemic. It was time. Every time I looked around, he was into something that was not positive. This kid is beyond spoiled, so I didn't understand what he was facing. I mean, a lot had changed since JW and I got divorced. He was acting out more, and I just didn't get it. JW and I decided that it may be best if my son lived with him. Besides, he is the only person our son feared. I was relieved, and my head was hurting. I needed him to be stable.

I had a conversation with his biological mom, and she was against him going down south. She felt it would be best if she and her mom stepped in. I was against that, but at this point, I needed a solution. He was getting in trouble in school daily and it was overwhelming. On his phone, I caught him smoking weed, and I was livid to see his behavior getting progressively worse. I was tired of New Jersey, and, honestly, I was tired of him. I hadn't had a chance to enjoy my daughter, and it was unfair.

Prince was saying that his behavior would continue to get worse, and that made me upset. He was on the phone with me most of the time my son was acting out. It was embarrassing and disappointing because my son is my everything; I had sacrificed so much for him. It was crazy trying to figure out, "Is this God, or is this my flesh?" I am always sure about the Word for other people. Prince had me ministering before the people often. I was pushing myself, even when I didn't want to. If he asked me to preach, I did it. I was very submissive—not because he complained that he had a bad ex-wife. It was just in me. I was on my way to Georgia, and it was so exciting for me.

While at the airport, Prince's ex-wife was in my inbox saying that he was still married. When I met him, he never said any of this. I thought he was single, with the way he described his situation. He said that once he is done, he is done. He erased his marriage from his mind because he hadn't seen or contacted his ex-wife since February of the previous year. I was literally about to have a panic attack because why was his wife bothering me? If this was his spouse, she should have been calling him, not me.

Oftentimes, he talked about things that she would do to him that he deemed as wrong. I just was listening because it was important to be attentive during this time in our relationship. I ignored her in the beginning. She kept sending messages. After I responded to her, her daughter was in my inbox telling me she didn't like the way I responded to her mother. My response was, "Your mother had no right to contact me. If she has a husband, she should deal with her spouse."

He said he didn't remember a lot of things. However, she contacted him prior to casting a net and looking for me as her way to reach out to him. The daughter went on about his character. She said he was a master manipulator and all he did was take people's money. "The life that you are used to is not something you're going to get from him," she said. At this point in life, I could take care of myself. I wanted to know why these people were so mad. Lo and behold, my heart started racing, and it became hard to receive anything from the two of them. Everyone seemed angry.

No one was acting like a lady or a leader. She is an apostle, and I expected her to have a woman-to-woman conversation with me. Instead, it was messy and childish. I was over it all. My stress level was increasing daily. I literally couldn't trust anyone around me at this point in my life. I was on my way to see Prince and I was happy. Seeing Prince made my day better. I was only going to be in Georgia for one day. I paid for the hotel for my baby and my mother. Our flights were so expensive because I booked them at the last minute. I didn't care about the money. I was so happy. I wanted something new, something special, and something different. He had wisdom and he was knowledgeable. I often told him, "Teach me, baby." I was born a teacher, and I love to be taught. Him teaching me was extremely sexy.

I loved that he taught me because we could do great things together. Two talented individuals can produce much together. I arrived in Georgia and pushed past the drama with a delayed flight, baby. The odds were against me—whew, chile—on this day. I finally arrived and was as late as ever. Prince hated the dress that I wore to the airport. He was very vocal about his thoughts and opinions. It was a pink, flowy dress that stopped an inch above my knee. It didn't show anything at all. In his words, a woman was not supposed to show skin. He acted as if he was 55 years old. My knees were showing, sir. After we checked in and got to the room, I freshened up and went to meet my family.

Prince looked so good. I was impressed because he was a country dude. He had on a clean white shirt and some ripped jeans with a fedora hat. I had bought him some nice shoes for his birthday, and he was wearing them. Prince was smelling good, and oh, baby, it turned me on. I was being myself, as I told him I would. My birthday was coming up, and I was expecting him in New Jersey in a couple of weeks. He cooked and set up the decorations. Baby, I had gotten me a winner, and it was not up for debate.

The menu consisted of fried chicken, corn, string beans, and dinner rolls. My prince cooked and served me. He had me sit down while he served me, and it was more impressive than one could imagine. I am a servant, so to be served, baby, was like wow. He gave me butterflies. I felt like a little girl in his presence. He fixed plates and catered to me. He made an announcement to his family introducing me and Maddy.

We watched a video that he created. It was funny. It was a video of his family and his brothers. At the end of the video, he instructed me to turn around. I was having a slow moment because I still didn't understand what was about to happen. He was on one knee asking me to marry him. I said, "Yes, baby." He said, "What?", being himself with his sense of humor. I said, "Yes," louder. I spoke loudly, but I tried to refrain from doing so. He hugged me and kissed me softly.

I asked his momma if I could call her "Momma." She said yes! His momma asked if she could see my ring. She thought it was small, and so did I, but it was an engagement ring. Prince said white people present two rings. I was so grateful for the effort; it was the extra mile that intrigued me. He was appreciating the woman that I am without long speeches. He was showing me why I called him Prince. He showed me that he valued me, and it made me feel golden. I felt like I should've been on The Golden Girls television show because in my head, I was living in a fairy tale. Heaven is a great place I haven't been to, but this feeling was so amazing that I didn't want it to end. He reassured me that he always got me. That meant he had my back.

He didn't believe in cheating, so I didn't have to worry about that. I don't know what prayer I prayed, but God, I was so thankful for the blessing that was upon me. I have God, and I love God. I used to cry in the tub asking God to send me love: "God, send me someone in human form who is going to match me; someone who is going to honor me and live a peaceful life with me." I believed in my heart, mind, and spirit that this was it.

We took pictures while John interviewed the guests. He was showing off, and I was sooo cheesy. No one gets my attention, so when someone has it, I am all gas and no breaks. You could see if I had a cavity because all my teeth were showing. I was smiling from here to Mars, and I was unapologetic about it. The public and private love was the greatest feeling, and nothing could make me change my mind.

I never had someone this spiritual and into me. I had dated men of God, but there was a lot that came with them. Come on, Jesus, with this love on top! The event was over, and Prince cleaned and put away the party items. I was a fiancé now, and I wanted to chill with my prince. I went back to his room and I wanted to be nasty. At this point, I was getting married, but with the way he made me feel, my desire was uncontrollable. He ordained me as a pastor months prior. I know, I know, but this woman was hot in her pants in this humanistic moment.

My flesh was weak for this one here. I'm not into sex all the time. I'm not the woman who has to have it. I love the idea of mental stimulation. Make love to me without touching me. I love the thought of denying myself to hear from God. I was alone with Prince, and I kept telling him how special he made me feel. At this point, I was trying to be fresh. I realized that only God could judge me. This flesh was weak, honey.

This apostle, this gentleman, reminded me of the promises of God. Whew, chile, I seriously need to be saved. I was in heaven; I didn't feel rejected. I felt as if I had a man after God's own heart, and he was disciplined. I had hit the jackpot. Wow, I don't have to worry, I thought. God promised us a son, and I never, ever wanted another child until I met him. I wanted to give him something he never had. In that moment, when my flesh was up to no good, he asked me, "If we have sex before marriage, what will our promise look like?" The promises of God are "yea" and "amen." He was serious about not having intercourse before marriage.

Tanesha, your flesh has to die, is what I was saying to myself. I stopped trying, and immediately, I felt convicted on my way back home. It doesn't take people to convict you when you know that you are wrong. Prince and John took us to the airport. On our way to the airport, while everyone was sleeping, he told me, "We've got this. We can make it happen, Tanesha, and do this thing called life together." Baby, I was confident and sure of what I was about to embark on.

He told me a real woman builds her house, so I started looking for a place to live. I honored him and who he was. I agreed with him. I felt like I could move mountains with him by my side. We arrived at the airport and we were on the other side. Prince took us to the international side. Unfortunately, we missed our flight, and it would now cost more money to get back home. I seriously didn't care because it was worth it for me. I don't play about my money.

When I returned home from the airport, I started looking for places to live. I refused to leave my husband by himself. This guy was an incredible man. No way would I leave my baby alone. It was all dead ends for me looking for a place to live in Georgia. No one had what we wanted. I couldn't find anything at all. Looking for places daily became so discouraging. I had my own place in New Jersey. I was too through with where I was. I wanted to get away from everything. I had said yes to marriage, so I was in agreement with whatever we decided as a couple.

I started looking into Tennessee. Prince was born and raised in Tennessee. I wanted to live in a place I had never been to. I wanted to buy a house in Tennessee. The options Tennessee offers are unheard of. You can submit an application, and someone will purchase the house for you. You pay them money to repay the loan, but the house belongs to you. That idea was awesome, and all you had to do was meet the criteria. I had recently set Prince up with my childhood friend to fix his credit. Prince wanted to set a date for the wedding immediately. Every day, Prince was organizing the wedding. All I had to do was show up. All we had to do was find a place to live and we were set. We did not believe in living together before marriage. If we were staying in Georgia, our best friend, John, would stay with his grandmother. If we were leaving to go to Tennessee, he would come with us.

John had made me look so good on my social media platforms. He was our public relations person and he was super smart. He operated Prince's ministry page, and we had mega ideas; all of us working together would be amazing. My niece, who I had guardianship over, told me she didn't want to come with us. That was cool with me; instead of a four-bedroom house, we could get a three-bedroom. Prince was so elated and said God had answered his prayer.

CHAPTER 7

I kept my place in New Jersey so my niece could stay there. Also, when I visited New Jersey, I would have somewhere to stay instead of being uncomfortable. I had a plan, and I planned on executing it. I had it all mapped out: my plans, my visions, and my goals. The life I wanted for Madison was mapped out as well. Prince often told me to worry about Madison only. That was hard because all of them were a part of me. When I met Prince, I told him that I had three children. I missed life being just me and Maddy. I felt like I neglected a part of my child by stretching and bending myself for ungrateful people. Now, it was time that I started pouring all of myself into her.

My sister-in-law from my previous marriage was having a baby. In 2022, I learned to mind my business. My ex-husband's sister wanted me to give her a baby shower. I decorated it for her. My staff was telling me not to give her one because of all the things she had done. I was so disappointed and angry with her silly drama. She started all this beef amongst people who were okay with me.

My heart said, "Throw her the baby shower. She's never had one before." Disclaimer: Our hearts are dangerous. Don't follow your heart. The heart is deceitful. I put my differences aside and helped her pick out a dress to wear to her baby shower. I was hosting it in my backyard. I gave her one rule for my house: Don't invite anyone who has messed with JW. Lo and behold, she told me afterwards that JW was flirting with someone he used to mess with at her baby shower.

You know what, it doesn't matter, but it's the principle of the matter. She then informed me that I needed to change my passcodes; that JW was in my phone reading my messages. I am careless with my debit cards and phone. I just leave them around at times. I lose them often. He was reading messages between me and Prince. Whew, chile, I was beyond tired of everything. This was the craziest thing ever.

This was my house—I didn't and wouldn't hide my stuff. I was overwhelmed with joy and about to get married. I was so tired of these controlling spirits. This was out of control. I wasn't ever enough for him, and that was fine, but he had to stop torturing me because it was driving me insane. He didn't have me, and deep down, he didn't want me, but he wanted to keep records of what I was doing. Why? No way was I going to keep allowing this. The drama continued to the point that it was out of control. I was mentally exhausted. The screaming and yelling were too much. I called my dad, and he said, "Maybe it's time you put a restraining order on him." He harassed Prince. He harassed everyone that I dated. I didn't want to, but at that point, I was about to lose my mind. He went too far again, so I called the police and made a report.

JW acted as if I was delusional. While on the phone with the police, they asked me questions like, "Did he ever beat you?" I said yes. They made the statement look like it was current, and it wasn't, but he said scary things to me. I was scared because he started acting crazy. I was not about to risk my life for anyone. Days went by before

I told his sister and his brother. My sister-in-law tried to call me and tell me about what he was doing. I told her I didn't want to know. I was moving on and escaping drama.

Days went by, and he called me like everything was normal. I decided to tell him I put a restraining order on him. He requested the report, and I felt crazy—like I was the enemy. I was just tired of the harassment. Enough was enough, and something happened at that moment. He felt like I betrayed him. He couldn't breathe. He was always starting trouble with me. I understand love. But at this point, it was tormenting me, and I couldn't bear it. I didn't want anyone popping up at my house unannounced. I don't desire to be micromanaged.

Prince and I discussed this, and he said that day was my first day of freedom. I was in agreement. Prince was supposed to fly up for my birthday, and now, he said he couldn't. I was so disappointed because my birthday means the world to me. I can't lie—I felt a way about him not showing up. He sent me some shades and said he would give me the rest of the stuff when he saw me next. I didn't like that, either, because if he was not present, he could at least send me my gifts.

I dropped the charges against JW after a few weeks. He was always there when I needed him, and I couldn't go through with it. Calling the cops was going against the code. I started my birthday on a therapist's couch. I was so in tune with trying to break the cycles. JW joined me because I wanted to create boundaries with him. I wanted to establish a co-parent relationship. We had history, and after the way he treated me, I couldn't ever return. I found a new love within me. It wasn't about

Prince. It was about honor. It was about me, finally.

The therapist stated that we needed more sessions. He decided we didn't have to go; he was okay with the decision for me to move on. This was the best birthday for me because he was present and available to have an adult conversation. I went to get beautiful and start my day. I went to dinner with my mom and stepdad. My sister-in-law went into labor and I had my godson on my birthday.

We all went to a classy restaurant, and I told my dad about Prince. He asked me questions, and I answered them. I told him I was moving, and he said he didn't want me to get married again just to get divorced. He told me I would look like the problem. I understood and agreed, and I told him I just didn't see anyone holding me back from my prince. I told my dad the date we set, and he was sad because he was going to be out of the country. I told him I loved him and we finished celebrating my birthday.

The joy of the Lord is my strength. My loved ones and I fasted and prayed for happiness, and all three of my spiritual sisters received what we prayed for. Every day, we talked about life. Prince was not a big talker, but he had a big mouth. That didn't make much sense to me. I told him he wouldn't last up north because our mouths are slick as well. It was funny and all good for me. Our wedding day was approaching, and I asked Prince if he could pay for me to get my hair done. He said no. He paid for the whole wedding, so I understood, but I didn't really understand: "I am your wife-to-be. Pay for my hair, please."

Prince had dealt with an older woman before— perhaps he didn't have to pay for her hair. I believe in your spouse paying for hair, manicures, and pedicures.

Does the spouse have to do everything? No! Prince had a lot of demands and thoughts about what I should do. I always made it clear that he needed to pay for the stuff he was demanding. You want my nails long? That's an extra fee—pay for it. While he was in Georgia, he and John were always going to the park. I was all the more excited to know that he and I were about to be at the park, chilling, being a family. They were always out together, and it was cool because I had a family man. We were all always talking to one another.

John's family was accusing him and Prince of having a relationship. I didn't pay it any mind. We were all best friends, and truth be told, John was telling me everything. I didn't have an inclination that it was true. I know Prince's ex-wife was calling every connection that they had. The divorce was finalized. She was spreading rumors to everyone, even John's family.

I was looking amazing, and my website had dropped. I had my own barcode and I was on top of the world with the image. I wanted to let every chicken be that and fly with the eagles. Prince loved me and he showed it daily. He often had a lot of worship services. I became so engulfed in building his ministry that I forgot my own. He told me that my ministry was secondary to ours. I'd been doing my ministry alone; therefore, I didn't mind him taking the lead.

He talked about me becoming a first lady. I hated the terminology, "first lady." I expressed to him that after the first lady, there's a second lady. We laughed and kept things moving. I was having services and not speaking on my platform. I gave others a chance to speak. Baby, everyone was trying to sabotage me. It was unbelievable to see. I did have three great speakers, but the rest of them were crazy. I never really spoke or prophesied to individuals on Facebook Live. For me, that was crazy because that's what people know me for.

I was going through the process of being public with my man. He made a video, and it was out that he and I were engaged. The people were going crazy—two powerful people were together and about to do damage in the kingdom of God. Everyone was congratulating me on the engagement. I expressed to people what he truly meant to me. I was still living and minding my own business.

My prophet friend said, "Don't marry him. He is battling with this spirit." He instructed me to go to God. I had already gone to God. My spiritual parents gave their blessings to our union. People who knew him said he was a great man. I had my spiritual mother's well wishes. My biological dad felt like Prince wanted my social media clout. It was all scary. Fear tried to grip me, and a prophet came and told me to release my fear. I didn't have anything to be afraid of.

Prince and I had a conversation, during which I told him I had never had a man around my daughter and it was a little scary for me. All she knew was her daddy. I was too grown to start introducing my babies to different men. He said, "I will be her dad." Very smooth... That made me feel a lot better because he was into us. When she would walk into my bedroom, Prince would talk to her on video chat. He was adjusting to the noises that she made. My dad be on point, and so does my ex-husband. We are all crazy, but we see well. I was going to get married, and I had found a place. Prince was consistent about us and

what he wanted. That made my heart glad. He was preaching, saying what a prince was supposed
to do for his queen. I was excited that he understood the language of the way a queen was supposed to be treated.

As I was looking for a house to live in, I expressed to him that I needed a big tub so he could wash me up like he said he would on his live streams. I am all into being catered to. The only difference is, I'm going to give it back to my spouse. I couldn't wait to give out massages and have candlelit dinners. I am extremely romantic, and so was he. I couldn't wait to show this side of myself.

We were about to head to Georgia. I had our rooms booked, and Maddy and I planned on staying for two additional days. I was so excited because we got to hang together. Prince would get to see how Maddy acts. Of course, she wanted to act shy. She had a lot to deal with. I got my hair done and checked on my son. He had just gotten suspended for taking marijuana to school. Forty-five-day suspension—whew, chile. I sent him to my sister's house. I had to figure out what I was doing with him. I was getting married.

My dress came in. It was too small, but my cousin managed to help me. My daughter's dress was fitting. I had my favorite people around me: my mom, my daughter, my cousins, my brother, my niece, my sister-in-law, my rider, and my bestie. It was so nice. The wedding would be at the hotel that I got engaged in. It was so intimate, and he made the best out of it being last minute. He cooked and decorated for me a second time. What wouldn't my Prince Charming do for me? I was beyond amazed at his talent. He was literally just like me.

I got dressed at the hotel, and someone called a bomb threat. Are you thinking what I was thinking? The wedding was delayed. The makeup artist canceled at the last minute. She took my deposit and blocked me on Instagram. I was all the way done with Atlanta. I found someone else in ten minutes, and she made me look bomb. I was on time for my wedding; it was okay. Prince made it simple, but cute. It was so sweet for me. The decorator canceled, and Prince did not let anything shake him.

My prince was adaptable and dependable, and it showed. It was amazing to watch. I was panicking. I did everything I was supposed to do. It was now time to meet my prince at the altar. My head was spinning, but I was sure of myself and my prince. I was dressed, and my cousins looked amazing in their dresses. I was about to say, "I do." He was waiting for me at the altar, and I would soon get to meet those who I only knew on social media.

CHAPTER 8

Prince said we would only spend $2,000.00 a piece for the house. He was getting put out of Sarah's house. Since we got engaged, she was upset. That was strange to me. However, I didn't want him to be homeless at all, so I gave the landlord our deposit. Prince sent $2,000.00 to me so I could hold it. The landlord accepted the money, and we were about to get our keys. I had some loose ends that I had to tie together before I moved. John wanted $300.00 for taking our pictures. I had to pay for that as well. Prince covered everything else. Everything looked good; however, John took the pictures with his phone. As long as the job was done, I was satisfied with the services. I would have preferred for him to use a professional camera, but with the way technology is set up, phones can get the job done.

Maddy and I were in Atlanta, Georgia, chilling until we had to leave. We all went out to eat: Maddy, our BFF, and Prince. We had money from the wedding, so I paid. I kept the money that we were given. Prince took us all out for frozen yogurt afterwards. We were having fun and enjoying one another. The both of us hadn't had sex in a while, so when we did, it was beautiful. I was married now, so I could legally have fun. It didn't go as planned, but I had the rest of my life to have sex, right?

We were about to leave because our flight was about to arrive. I was so excited to get home to pack my house for our new life. Prince always wanted me to look a certain way. I threw away a lot of stuff because he said I had too much. I asked Prince to come and help me drive to Tennessee because it was a long trip from New Jersey. He said there were witches waiting to kill him in the region. I didn't say much because I respected the God in him.

My son was transiting with my sister and mother. I transferred everything because I was leaving, and my son was getting on my last nerve. It had been a journey, and I was ready to embark on bigger, greater, and mega. My seasonings and hair products were about to launch. Things were coming together for me and my new family. I often told my momma-in-law that I would have Prince until the end of time. She was happy, and she loved me. I mean, what's not to love? I was true to myself, loyal, and honest. I am very forgetful, but when I remember, I remember. The family was very chill and relaxed. The days of being in New Jersey were coming to a close. I was about to rent a trailer to go on the back of my truck.

My niece's mother, who is my rider, decided that she would help me drive to Tennessee. She lives in Georgia, so I could take her home after we got to Tennessee. I said I would set my new house up, then return to get my daughter. I didn't want to do it all, and she was there, looking at me. Maddy was used to her Wi-Fi and television, and I wanted to have things set up just the way she liked it.

Prince didn't want anyone in our new home. I had to get my rider a hotel because I wouldn't inconvenience my niece and let them sit in the car. They needed a shower, so I put them up in a hotel for a couple of hours. I didn't want to tell her what he said because to me, it was inappropriate. I did what I had to do to keep the peace. Prince had already gotten the house together when I went to drop off my niece in Georgia. He was upset because I was going to Atlanta. I explained to him that my rider had helped out with gas and helped me drive. He did everything quickly. I stayed with him for two days, and then I was back on the road to get Madison. He said it was all dumb, and I asked him, "Did you give me gas money?" He looked puzzled. I cooked an omelet with spinach, eggs, and mushrooms. I made sure I went food shopping so that he could have groceries while I was gone. He loved the meal and said he could have it every day. That made me smile because he was into my food.

I got back on the road, and he told me I did too much. I laughed and kept pushing because that's what we do as women. I was in New Jersey for two weeks, and then I went back to Tennessee to be with my husband. I missed him like crazy, and I wanted him to know that I was coming right back. I handled all my business and went back home. I was out of the house in Tennessee, but I still paid my bills. I was on my way back home to cook for my prince. I made him shrimp alfredo, as it was something he wanted for the first meal. Prince posted on social media, "It's something about home-cooked meals."

I drove to Tennessee and set Maddy up in her room. I was nervous because my baby was in a new environment. We showered and laid down. At this point, my back was killing me so badly. I asked Prince if he could rub it and he said no. I said, "Prince, I just got done driving 17 hours, and you can't rub my back?" I was in tears. Yes, I can be a spoiled brat, but dang. "I was literally driving because I missed you," I told him. He said that I was trying to manipulate him because he told me he wouldn't massage my back when I was in New Jersey. I drove, and my family was pissed because they felt he should have helped me drive back. I was still pushing because it wasn't about them. I believed what he said, and I wasn't arguing with his relationship with God.

I was trying to relax for the first three days of being home after driving, but Prince wanted to talk to me. Baby, he had a list: I, as a woman, needed to get up at 5:00 in the morning and get my house in order. He said he didn't want to see a man cleaning his house when he had a wife. I was offended because I had only been there for three days. I listened and started getting up to clean at 5:00. My daughter wasn't in school, and I had the energy, but I also didn't have the energy at the same time. I just wanted peace to remain in my home. I thought to myself, This is crazy as hell. Before, I didn't have to clean because my kids did all the domestic stuff around the house. I obeyed and did as my husband wanted. Every day, he wanted me to clean, and the house wasn't dirty.

At that moment, he was comparing me to his ex-wife. He kept saying what he was used to. I told him not to compare me because while I could compare him to others, I didn't. For instance, my ex would have never let me drive alone as his wife. I didn't say that, though. I did explain that his ex-wife and I were two different people. The exhaustion from cleaning up after Maddy is a lot. I went from having an army to it just being me and her. I was very privileged. Do you know that I left all my help? Now, I had to find a space where I could function and be productive, and it could take a minute. I was unwinding and trying to learn Prince, myself, and Maddy. I was learning Maddy all over again because she was in a new place. I was learning Prince because we were together now—no more phone connecting us.

This was the real deal. The truth was, my nerves were bad as heck. I was falling and being all the more clumsy. All of this was something new, something fresh, something different. I had to catch up; it was a huge adjustment. I was in a place in my life where I was ready to embrace it, but there was nothing wrong with Prince helping me. So, here I was, being Superwoman. When I left New Jersey, I told him I no longer wanted to be Superwoman anymore. I wanted to be a normal woman, but that was impossible because I didn't have a normal calling. I don't have normal children, and I'm not normal. Everything about me is peculiar. I took out trash and cleaned up daily. This was beyond me because I don't take out trash.

He only ate once a day, so I didn't have to cook often. John was aggravated with Prince because his mouth was crazy. It was like he was being verbally abusive. John would often say that he didn't come to Tennessee to be abused. He could have stayed in Georgia for all of that. Prince was a different dude. Prince then started talking about my weight, which was an absolute no-no for me. I gained weight during the pandemic, but he married me anyway. Was he trying to show off? Was he just being a kid? Either way, it didn't feel good. I had a conversation with him about that.

After he talked about that, he wanted to talk about his ex. I was all the way confused. Before, Prince had said she wasn't a good wife, but now, she was. Was he bipolar? We were married now. Why was the conversation about her? I already told him I didn't want to hear her name.

"Well, she used to do that, and that made me mad..." Great information, but I didn't want to hear about her. This was a new chapter and a new beginning.

His tongue was beyond piercing, and I didn't understand how he was so uplifting to people, yet negative toward me at the same time. None of this made sense to me. When he wanted to watch television, he would say, "Give me the remote." In my head, I was like, This dude has got to be crazy. My elevator don't go to the top floor, and I always told him that. He was so demanding; it was ugly. Prince wanted me to drop everything to cater to his needs and wants. He wanted juice immediately. Like, huh? I don't mind serving my spouse, but you've got to say it better, dude. I was thinking, What the heck did I just get myself into? I would have a conversation with him, and he would tell me to close his door. Dude, this is our room, and I paid my rent this month. I didn't like his weight "jokes" or him talking down to me at all.

Then, he would go on Facebook and say he had the best wife ever. I am not into public success and private stress. No way. I was all the way baffled, and I felt estranged. I would cook for him, and he would say my food was nasty. I rushed to serve him, and he simply told me that I didn't have to rush and do things quickly. In all honesty, he taught me how to serve a man. I started to pay attention to how I was serving him. It was a plus, but his delivery was horrible. Then, he would say my attitude was bad. Dude, you haven't seen an attitude yet.

He and I were doing ministry, and it was great. I just needed him to be a man of his word. You have to practice what you preach. It was continuous. His disposition was nasty. I was trying to look past his flaws because I have my own. I was saying, "Yes, sir," and "Thank you." I was literally trying to set the tone for a wife building her house. If he did something, I would tell him he was the best. When you are a wife, you plant seeds, and eventually, the seed will grow. I believe in planting seeds. I thought that one day, his mind would catch up to me planting the seed.

CHAPTER 9

Thanksgiving was approaching, and I knew that I was pregnant. My body was spreading and I was getting questioned by him every day. He wanted to know how I was feeling. He wanted to know if I felt pregnant. He was so concerned; it was beautiful to watch. I took a pregnancy test and it was positive. I was so happy. Prince was acting crazy, but maybe he was testing my gangster or my personality. Either way, I didn't like it. God showed me my son before I married Prince. The excitement was in God keeping His word. Prince was a different character now that I was with child. He watched what I ate daily. He was not playing about his son.

I was so used to being rough that I was trying to adjust to having a baby inside of me. All I wanted to do was give my husband something he'd never had before. I was growing, and our best friend was having dreams about our son. Prince was getting prophecy that I was having twins. I was so amazed at God keeping His word. My belly was growing, and he was willing to do whatever. He didn't want me to lift a finger. Prince started experiencing sickness. He was vomiting, and I was glad it wasn't me. He always wanted to feel the symptoms. I don't ever remember getting sick with Maddy. Being by myself, I knew it would be difficult getting sick and having to function with my special needs child. Yes, Prince, take on my sickness because God knows best.

My daughter was starting school, and I was relieved because I got to rest. My son was growing, and my husband was amazing at this time. He was my dietician and doctor. Prince reassured me and said this would be my best pregnancy. I was in agreement because he was so attentive. I couldn't wait until my first doctor's visit. Weeks went by, and I started bleeding. Prince was on the internet telling me that this was normal; I would be fine. I went to the bathroom and it stopped. I was hyped to no return and he was so stern, like he was pregnant. I started bleeding again; this time, there were blood clots. I sent pictures of the blood to him, and he knew I had lost our son. I was devastated.

Then, the pain began. Days went by, and the bleeding continued. I went to the emergency room, and there was no baby or pregnancy. I'd only had one pregnancy before, and now, I had lost my son who we'd prayed so hard for. I came back home, and I had to tell my husband that the baby was gone. I cried before I got to him and shut down. I stopped answering his phone calls. I just didn't know how to process this. I walked in the door and told him I lost the baby; nothing was even coming up in the emergency room. He didn't say anything. At that moment, he was devastated, too. I couldn't tell because I was carrying my baby, and what I felt was rage. Prince stopped talking, and so did I. I was trying to get through the day. Every day, we had baby talk, and he asked questions. Now, our conversation was limited because I was in pain.

This was my husband, and I didn't know what to say or if I should say anything at all. He was in his own feelings. So, weeks were going by, his face looked different, and I was still in my feelings. I didn't discern what he was facing. I didn't think it affected him, but it did. I just knew I took a bullet, and this wound didn't feel good. One day, I went to him and asked him if we could talk about it. He said no. At that moment, I was about to have a breakdown. I needed my husband to hold me. I desired affection, and he wasn't affectionate. I needed him to say, "Okay. We will try again." I needed him to be vocal, and all I received was silence.

I continued to go live on social media when I felt like it. I wasn't consistent because I wasn't stable. I was trying to figure out what had just happened and why. Prince was very vocal with Maddy. He became very compassionate about Maddy. He wanted to know if she was okay. He was concerned about her well-being. He was making sure she was good, and that was great. In these moments, I appreciated the concern, but I needed my husband. I needed him in a way that I didn't even understand. I wanted something that wasn't in him, or something that he wasn't ready to display with me.

I was sad and feeling hopeless, like I wasn't a woman. It was hard for me to reproduce—or was it simply not meant for me to reproduce with him? My analytical mind was racing. My husband and I were doing ministry, and he was selling his jewelry. I was super proud of him because he stayed occupied. I still had to be a mom, a wife, and a first lady, and I couldn't understand this space I was in. Maddy's smile brightened up my day every day.

CHAPTER 10

It was December, and I started Christmas shopping. Prince said it was the family custom that we buy everyone something for Christmas—family buys us gifts, and we buy them gifts. I was shopping for them. Prince was still not vocal about the miscarriage, and that was killing me. He was in bed all day and I was in the living room. He was always in bed because he suffered from migraines. I decided that I would initiate a conversation and tell him I felt a disconnect between us. I would often talk about us having a baby, and that annoyed him. I had no idea how he felt because he didn't speak about it.

He had his private conference that he wanted me to pay him to attend. When I was in New Jersey, I could attend the conferences for free. Now that we were married, I had to pay, so I told him I was not attending. I was not going to pay my husband for his knowledge. Why would I do that? "If you want to make me be this grand preacher, teach me. Anyone who wants to truly see you succeed helps you grow and become. Since I have to pay you $50.00 per class, I'm not attending." He was serious, and so was I. I was really trying to figure this out. He used my seasoning and didn't pay. I bought groceries and he didn't pay. I don't know what kind of marriage he was used to. I don't charge my spouse to use my stuff.

My husband had this thing where I was not allowed to touch his stuff. I was in agreement that I would not touch anything. Prince was touching everything that belonged to me, and I was trying to understand. I really didn't care if he touched my stuff. However, I did care about him wanting me to respect his stuff and him not respecting mine. I'm far from petty. If I do something, you're going to know that I did it.

I got sick. Maddy was sick, too, and I felt like death had just hit me. I stayed in her room because Prince and our best friend were fine. I didn't want to make anyone ill. I was not about to give them what I had. I was asking Prince, "Can you please take care of me?" He said, "I'm no doctor. Go to the emergency room." For three days, I was down and out. He never checked on us. He used to say to me that Maddy was not my only responsibility. She was now, because in these moments, there were only us two. She and I had one another's backs. I was far away from home with no one. I didn't want to call anyone because it was embarrassing to tell this story. That's how I felt in the beginning. It was too early for him to be giving me his tail to kiss. I don't even think I showered; that's how weak I was. The fourth day, I felt better, and I woke up to dishes and cans overflowing from the sink. I was confused because I had been down. I cleaned and didn't say one word because this was the same dude who said women should never go to bed with dishes in the sink. I cleaned and didn't complain.

Christmas was approaching, and I wasn't excited. He kept asking me to get him an Apple computer. I had just opened up the largest business ever. I couldn't afford to take care of all three of my children and get him an Apple computer. I kept telling him, "No. I'm not getting that." Every year, I was always in the Christmas spirit. I love Christmas and birthdays. This Christmas, I wondered if I was in the right setting. What did I just get myself into? He kept telling me all I had to do, but I had my own custom celebration that I always did. I was willing to bend because he was my husband. Whew, chile.

He said that we would exchange gifts with his family. I was so aggravated because it seemed like I was buying most of the gifts. I cooked brunch and set everything up in a cute way. I was frustrated because everything around me was geared towards him. Every day, I found pen marks on my couches. I asked myself, Is this dude writing on my brand-new furniture? I was livid because I would have destroyed my kids for the same thing he was doing. It seemed like this apostle was being malicious towards my stuff.

He was throwing groceries in the trash. I was looking at him stupid because the number one rule was to give away food, not throw it away. He was throwing away fresh meat, and when I asked why, he said it was bad. "Baby, let me take this back to the store instead of you trashing it," I suggested. It meant nothing to him because he wasn't in the grocery store twice a week. I was beyond fed up with this apostle. He was steadily preaching and speaking about life to people while his wife was in the other room on the edge. He had a word every other day, if not every day.

He despised the way I preached; therefore, he was hard on me. He wanted me to preach a word that would make people happy. I am not that type of preacher. Whatever the Holy Ghost says, I move with God. He was telling me my messages were getting better, but I was disconnected from the people.

John was running our StreamYard, and I had to pay him $100.00 a month to do so. I was still waiting on wedding pictures from him. Finally, I received them, and there were 32 pictures for $300.00. I was about to blow up, in all seriousness. These two con artists didn't just play me, I thought. All along, they were partners in business. Prince had encouraged me to get the highest, most expensive photography package.

On top of everything that we were already going through, my husband wouldn't touch me at all. He didn't show me affection. Newlyweds are supposed to be all over one another. I was sleeping on the couch because I didn't know what was happening. Something didn't feel normal or right to me.

I went live one day, and John became offended by the fact that I wanted to help with his business. I was telling people about my non-profit organization. I was nervous, and my voice was very shaky while I talked. They both made me nervous because they were critiquing my work. John yelled and screamed at me, telling me what I needed to do as an entrepreneur. I had been making money before I met them. I had been on my own before I met them. I had connections before I met them. He didn't know me at all. He said I would go to jail due to me telling the people wrong information. He kept going and going, and the more he went on, I became angrier. He told me I was better than that, and he expected me to go and sell my products to the people.

I told the people that if they needed help, I had a team that could help them. John went on to say that he didn't work for me, and "Don't be telling people that." I never said his name or anything, but he went off. I sat quietly. My husband came out of the room laughing, and in that moment, I knew that I was displaced. No one talks to me like that. He didn't come out of the room to tell him, "Chill. I will take over." He didn't say anything. He came out to laugh. There had been no intimacy, no affection, and no love, and now, he wouldn't even defend me. Enough was enough, and to laugh was an indication of the immaturity that lay within. I often called him immature, and he would say I had a small vocabulary. "I am far from immature; let me go to Facebook to ask the people."

The people were manipulated like me, and honestly, he presented himself well publicly. It's funny because I would go to jail for telling people things like, "A non-profit is not for profit." My husband was on social media lying to people about money and saying that everyone was going to be wealthy. John wasn't yelling at Prince for being a predator. It was the private encounters that I couldn't believe.

Christmas was a few days away, and I had gotten all I was going to get for my husband. John had as many gifts under the tree as I did. I was feeling uneasy about the way he spoke to me, so now, I was mute because I don't do well with disrespect. I didn't want to talk or do business. The very good intent went unnoticed.

I lost my debit card and my website, so I was angry. All the money I had spent was down the drain. John was unbothered, and so was my husband. These dudes had just gotten me and my money, and it was all just okay, apparently. I wasn't asking him to do anything for free, but I wanted to revisit this because I needed my website. Nothing was said or done about it!

It was Christmas Eve, and John started a new job. He was working now, and the house was silent. I couldn't take it. I felt like a roommate in my own home. My mother-in-law would come over, and my husband was the best at pretending. A predator can put on a good show. He was trained to do so. The house was still quiet. I made it my business to leave two days after Christmas. My daughter was doing amazing in school, but I was failing in my marriage. I didn't care because I planned my exit quietly, and at this point, I didn't know if Prince and our best friend, John, were lovers or what.

On Christmas morning, I was up because I was used to the kids going nuts over toys. Maddy is so spoiled; she had been getting gifts every day of the week as we shopped. Therefore, her time spent opening presents was short. At 1:00 p.m., she had just started opening gifts. I cooked waffles and eggs and had fruit. My husband was in bed, and after he got up, he threw the food in the trash because he said I'd left it out. More food wasted, but whatever. I will never understand that.

I finally opened my presents, and Prince had seriously gotten me and John the same number of gifts. My husband was not satisfied with his presents at all. I got him customized pens that said, God don't miss. I purchased him a popcorn machine, boxers, socks, customized towels with his initials on them for his live streams on social media, an organizer for his glasses, and a holder for his chargers and phone. My husband came up with the idea that we should stuff stockings. I purchased the stockings and began to follow instructions. Can I tell you that the only ones who followed through with the plan were me and John? My husband never placed anything in our stockings. It was clear he is not a man of his word.

CHAPTER 11

My husband wanted an Apple computer, but I refused to spend $2,000.00 on him. I had spent enough, and I felt crazy for spending anything at all. Days went by and I said nothing to either of them. I felt like I was deceived by words; once I got to Tennessee, the actions didn't match. I was having health problems. My son was acting crazy, and JW stated that it was because I left. I was not buying that because he was acting up even while I was there. I hired a team to come move me out. Two days after Christmas, I was heading to New Jersey for a family gathering, and also to return home. This marriage was not for me, and I was lied to. He didn't want to purchase anything without going half on the payment. At this point, he was a half nigga.

Meanwhile, John only paid for trash collection and Wi-Fi. He went from our BFF to his best friend. I was not claiming anyone who treated me like this. No. That was unacceptable to me. I had to pay for a car note, two homes, life insurance, light bills, and food for my children. Somebody was silly, and it wasn't me.

I woke up early to prepare for the move. Maddy was up, and I was in the kitchen. That day, John was talking to me, asking me where I was going so early. I told him I was moving because I didn't know if they were lovers or what. My husband woke up and told me to go to the bedroom so he and I could talk. I broke down so badly and started crying, telling him I needed him to be my husband. He said he needed me because he was going through the loss of our child. He rubbed my back and said I was the best thing that had ever happened to him; I couldn't leave him. He told me he loved me and I couldn't do this to him.

At that moment, I felt crazy. I had a hair appointment waiting for me in New Jersey. I also had this U-Haul scheduled. I was leaving because my eyes couldn't be playing tricks on me. He wanted to rub me—finally, some affection. I was trying to get myself together mentally. He told me he was having flashbacks and he didn't know how to deal. He said he covered me in prayer. God revealed to him that he was wounded in this area. I didn't want to hear that. I showered and calmed down. He told me all he wanted was me. I believed him and asked him if I could go to New Jersey. He asked me when I would come back home. I told him I would be back in seven days. My daughter had school in Tennessee, which she enjoyed.

I forgot all the things I was doing prior to moving. I had already scheduled for everything to be turned off. The water and light bills had to get out of my name. I was getting everything out of my name.

At that moment, I was emotional as heck. I loved him, and I realized that people have struggles. My husband said that I was experiencing miscarriage grief. I probably was. I told him he never wanted to go out to dinner anymore; all he wanted to do was lay in bed and go live on social media. Where was our relationship? I couldn't make this up. I could have been grieving, but there was some lack on his behalf. I was not used to this life at all. I'm used to being treated well. If anyone mistreated me, I knew how it was supposed to be. I didn't cut off all those men who took me on $400.00 dates to be treated like trailer trash.

You have to work in marriage—I understand that.

Marriage is ministry. If the pandemic was the reason that we couldn't go outside, we could create an environment in the house and celebrate with one another. This was not what I envisioned for myself. Madison was in school, and we could hang out while she was at school. But to be newly married and just be looking at one another? No way. I was not having it at all. He wasn't convincing me, so I went to pick up the U-Haul. He came outside and told me to take it back, and I did. I returned and he wanted to have sex, but I didn't because sex clouds your judgment. I packed light. I was coming back home in seven days. I just needed to get my hair done and see my son and niece.

CHAPTER 12

As soon as I reached New Jersey, I caught Covid and stayed in New Jersey for one month. Maddy and I were very sick. Her dad had Covid and came to hug her, and we caught it from him. While I was in New Jersey, God was speaking to me. I was dreaming and hearing from God like crazy. I was dreaming of myself having sex with a woman. In the dream, I was talking to someone who was very close to me once upon a time, asking her why she didn't tell me she was in love with me. We would have been in a relationship. I was so paranoid because I had never thought about being with someone of the same sex before. I called my prophet brother, and he said God was trying to show me what I was around.

When I was in Tennessee, I heard God, but he was loud in New Jersey. I was doing my live streams, sick and all. I was anticipating my live streams on social media. The funny part about all of this is that I had never felt so strong, even being sick. I recovered, and Prince was not trying to have me home unless I was Covid-free. The truth was that I missed this dude, and hopefully, things would be different. Time would tell if I was tripping.

He released an ASMR video, and he looked suspect in the video. He was fanning his hands, and to me, he looked like he could be gay. Oh, my God. What did I get myself into? My husband wasn't ever around gangsters, and he wasn't a hard man. He was gentle. That wasn't an indication that he was gay, though. Keep reading!

Maddy and I recovered, and I had the strength to go home and deal with everything at hand. My husband said that if he didn't love me, he would have let me leave. He was rough with his words. I kept telling him he couldn't pluck my wounds. Plucking wounds can cause an infection in my body. That was not a good method. He began to tell me his dislikes about me. He wanted me to get up every day and get dressed and beat my face like the women do in The Real Housewives of Atlanta.

Concerning me leaving, he told me that all my actions were like a street woman's. He should have researched me, because at any cost, I will remove myself from anything that is not good for me and my baby. When you have experienced much, you will not tolerate junk or mediocrity. I was more than the image he was trying to paint. I'm no street woman, but I have survival skills that I've learned from the urban neighborhood to wake me up in a crazy situation.

Baby, if he wanted that life, he should have moved up north where I had help. I was trying to figure myself out in this space. He hated the fact that I wore tights around the house. I told him my clothes were too expensive to be in the house chilling in them. I told him to take me somewhere—then, I would change my attire. Most dudes don't mind tights. He is not like most, and I understand that. "Let me know what you like so I can keep it tasty and do what you desire," I told him. I am not totally busted, but I'm not dolled up around the house. He had expectations, and I wasn't meeting them. I literally had to drive miles to get that out of him.

He wanted me to be different, and I wanted the same for him. I was ready to go home to Tennessee. I purchased $300.00 worth of clothes for Madison. Her birthday was coming up, and I was going to let her have a ball. Her dad was coming, and she would stay with him. She had a ball! It was cool. I went home the next day. As soon as I got home, we had food waiting for us. I was so happy that he was bending for us. He purchased bulks of detergent for our clothes. He purchased bulks of tissue. He was on his job, doing the things he was supposed to do before we got married. That was an agreement that we had: If you don't pay bills, then we should be loaded with household products. I bought all the furniture; the least he could do was get supplies for the house. Everything that I had was brand new. I had just purchased new furniture and painted my house.

I was not being unreasonable. I know I wasn't being unfair at all. He was so happy to see me, and it was the same feeling for me. We lay in bed, and I was so happy to be with him. I missed his phony self. I did not have high expectations for what he would deliver, but I was willing to get the full story like a reporter to free women. I loved my husband, and I wished I was being delusional. At least then, I could say it was me and not him. He had rearranged our home; it was now full of his stuff. The kitchen table that we purchased was his desk, so my daughter could no longer eat at the table. The kitchen had a television in it. The living room was for his jewelry, and our room had my office in it.

I was all for making money, but he didn't consult me for anything, and that bothered me. I saw my brand-new machine in the trash. I had never used it, and it was a five-in-one heat pressing machine. I could have sent it back to Amazon or exchanged it. Instead, he threw it in the trash without telling me or asking me. I asked him about it, and he said he had already told me. I am the take-back queen. I would have heard that. I was so frustrated by this garbage ministry that he had. It seemed like only my stuff went in the trash. I was paying attention. I went to New Jersey and gained the strength to deal with whatever I was walking into.

My ultimate goal was to have a good marriage. If my marriage couldn't be good, and if I was on an assignment to expose him, I would do that as well. My prophet friends already told me what God was saying. My response to them was, "I'm no super savior, but if I have to go back to freeing leaders and women, I am willing." I didn't want to be on an assignment because I loved this man. If I didn't, I wouldn't have done all of these things. I was seriously in love with him. I wanted my mind to be playing tricks on me. I wanted to be delusional. That would kill and override my godly insight.

I kept seeking God because this was my life. Prince turned things around being from all about him to all about us. I was on flyers with him. I was being honored for Valentine's Day. I understood his temporary fits. I did have one issue, though: While I was in New Jersey, this lady called me and told me I was jealous of my husband. I was on the phone trying to figure out who she was talking to. She confirmed that she was talking to me, and then she proceeded to tell me that she didn't want my husband. I can own anything, and baby, God was dealing with my response. She didn't have any clue what she was talking about.

I didn't think he wanted her. I knew he loved me, and I loved him back. She told me that everything about me was jealous, and she went to my Facebook page to confirm the spirit I was operating in. "You always call him Prince," she said. I was laughing because I called him Prince every day. After Prince and I had a conversation about what happened, he put the woman on his platform to preach. I was looking at him crazy because this prophet liar had just come for me. I confronted him, and he said I had to shake people off. Now, I can shake stuff off, but he should not have invited her on our platform. That is not loyalty. I was the one who had to cut people off for calling him names.

Man, this can't be my life right now, I thought. I was listening to the voice of God and I didn't care about anyone's judgmental opinions. I was staying on course to get the meat of the story and help out in this woman's battle. I knew that staying would come with wounds. I would gain new scars. I told God I could handle it. I might have to cry, but at that point, nothing would destroy me. I was enduring, sis, cuddling and watching movies with my husband. I was literally chilling. He was walking on eggshells, and it's not like I'm a compulsive complainer. We both had our ways, and the real me had not come out yet because I can go from zero to 100 really quickly—or so I thought.

I was changing for the better. I had been letting people slide, not telling them how I felt. I had been taking life with a grain of salt and just letting people show their true colors. It's amazing how people really flaunt their stuff. I was doing ministry with the prince. We were on our job, pouring into people daily. After we ended the live stream on social media, he went to sell jewelry. He was doing his thing, and I wasn't stopping him. All I desired was for him to have balance and live a life that he enjoyed.

On the days when I kicked him out so I could clean and he could live, he and John got Covid shots so he would feel safe being outside. He did everything with this dude. There was no normalcy here at all. He started going out daily to handle business with John. Valentine's Day was approaching, and all I wanted was some smell-goods. Prince went out and got me a bike. I could have licked his face, I was so happy. He was not for the germs, and I didn't want to hear his mouth, so I didn't. I was so happy. I was just thinking about that bike, and here he went and bought it for me. What he didn't know is that I had given away my bike before moving, and it was the same color. He also gave me perfume. I was elated.

Then, he and John went out to get their nails done. I went to buy him a cake, two pairs of jeans, and a game for Valentine's Day. I purchased him some steak, and we cooked together. He was a beast at cooking. I understand why he didn't like my food. He was better at cooking. After we cooked, he went live, and sometimes, I'm shy. I love to live in the moment. Everything is not for everybody, and I wanted to smile privately, but this social media hype? He is into it, big-time. I went along with my husband and made vows to follow him. He said this was the time that we were living in.

Social media is such a distraction. He wakes up and that's the first thing he does. Whew, chile, we are not the same. Our mentalities are different, and the more I was home, the more I saw it. John's birthday was coming up, and we were planning on going to Vegas. Pay attention, please.

CHAPTER 13

Life was good, and I was going to New Jersey for the weekend for my Mommy's birthday. I could get my hair done and see my son. Every time I was in New Jersey, I had my son. I did what I could. I always made sure he was good. I sent him money every day. Prince always had a problem with me jumping for my kids. Prince had to take me to the airport, and he had my truck. He said he was going home to park my truck because he didn't play with people's stuff, which I knew was a lie. He played with people's stuff, but he didn't want anyone to touch his stuff. I drove myself and had enough gas in my car to make the trip back and forth.

I landed in New Jersey and was ready to get my hair snatched. I was on my way. Our plane ride was funny. I had never flown with Spirit, and I felt like I was on Soul Plane. It was funny and ghetto. My mom picked me, my niece, and her mom up from the airport. We ran around like chickens with our heads cut off. Everything for this party was delayed, decorations and all. Mommy never said she wanted all of this at her party. She is so extra, but I spoiled her, so I have to live with it, right? I was getting my son and my niece together. I was so overwhelmed by the amount of work that we had to get done. I was going to fulfill it all because you only get one mom. I went to sleep dead tired, and woke up the next day alert and ready for the party. I love parties.

Mommy was over the moon, and she invited everyone to hang out with her. There were thirteen of us in total. I got to see my godson, and it made my heart glad. My son was happy, and so was my niece. I drive a Lexus truck, and Lexus Link located my car at a hotel. I had just gotten off the phone with Prince, and he said he was going to sleep. I called him immediately, because now, I was mad as heck. He answered, and I asked, "Why is my car's location saying you are at a hotel?" "Baby, I went to get your car washed." But the FaceTime call was showing him in front of the hotel. He was actually at the hotel for three hours. My blood was boiling and I wasn't understanding. "How do you get out of the bed, put the car in reverse, then drive, and don't tell me what's going on with my vehicle? You just said 'good night' to me." Prince told me that I was beautiful, always. That was something that he always said to me. This particular time, he did not.

I was ready for the next day to come because I wanted to go investigate. I was about to search high and low for my answers. Then, he told me he was at a restaurant. I couldn't get him to take me to lunch, but as soon as I left the state, he was outside with his best friend, John. Make this make sense to me, Apostle. I got off the plane with a huge attitude. He was late getting me from the airport as well. I was really heated because now, my baby was in the cold while he had our wheels. He never called to say, "I am late, baby, but I'm coming." I had to call him. For 30 to 45 minutes, I was out there wondering if I was going to go to jail that night. Maddy always saves me, seriously.

They pulled up, and he didn't help me with my bags. His BFF was telling us to hurry up, and I was furious. I left my brand-new rugs behind because no one helped me with my bags. He was something else. As I got into the car, my Lexus truck was on empty with the gas light on. I am not in college, and I don't drive a beat-down car. I hadn't cleaned it because I was used to getting my car washed by workers. However, my truck is nice. He pulled over to the gas station and put $10.00 worth of gas in my vehicle. I started shaking my leg. Then, he had the nerve to put regular gas in my Lexus. I was all the way done. I walked in the store and put $30.00 in my gas tank. No way would we make it with that amount driving one hour from the airport home.

I couldn't wait for John to get out of the car. I was going to tell him that he was a bum. Who does this? Only a bum. I am not into negative conversations with my spouse. However, this was not acceptable. We had never had an argument. Had he consulted me about my vehicle, I would have given him instructions on what not to do. I was in another state being played.

While, chile. Are you ready?

Then, I checked my mileage. He had driven my car three hours away to his brother's event. I only knew this because I was timing my oil changes. I now had to get one because he taken my car for a six-hour drive and didn't say a word. I was pissed and I wanted to cuss because that is how I get myself and my daughter from point A to point B. I had just spent money on my momma, and now, I had to get my tires rotated and an oil change the next day.

He proceeded to say, "I wasn't missing my brother's event for anybody." I said, "If you had told me, I would have told you to go get an oil change." I told him he was a selfish bastard. No way would I not communicate when it came to someone else's stuff. Not only was he a liar; my car was still dirty. Where is the lie? "I don't ride in your car. Your best friend always has it," I reminded him.

I went to turn on my computer and the screen was black. I asked him what happened. He was cleaning and broke it. He said he would pay for my oil change if I wanted. My response? "Oh, yes, you will." I don't know what kind of country mentality this is. I would never take advantage of anyone. Truth be told, he doesn't even like my truck. It was convenient because he needed it. That sounds like an opportunist to me. I was about to get into our bed, and he wanted to kiss. No. Kiss yourself, because baby, I feel some type of way. I don't like to feel taken advantage of. I have a nice personality. I also have a not-so-sweet one. I could only get affection when he was wrong.

First, my truck, then my laptop and the hotel location. He told me two different stories: He went to clean my car. Then, he went to get some food. Whew, chile, I wanted answers—now. I went to sleep and woke up alert. I was on my way to the hotel. I wanted some answers. I was so desperate that I was willing to pay for information. He told me I was acting insecure—he could save that for a little girl who didn't know any better. I may be insecure if someone says I am big. If you say something about my weight, I am a bit insecure, but I am not insecure concerning anything else. I am the type that if the shoe fits me, I am wearing it.

No one is going to add to my story because I know me. I am so heartbroken to see that this man went from having my back to only caring about himself. I went to the restaurant and it was hard to get information out of the people. Lexus Link located the car and told me my location, and boom, my husband was lying. I didn't have proof of who he was with besides John, but someone was lying. Why he would marry me is what I was trying to figure out: Why do you think wealthily, yet act foolishly? I came in from getting my oil changed and handed him the receipt. He sent me the money on Cash App and had the worst attitude. I didn't care about anything concerning his attitude.

NO one checks people who act like him. NO one, and that's why he has an issue with accountability. He wanted to grab my face and tell me he loved me and he would never cheat on me. Man, you are cheating with your phone. You're on that device more than you are attentive to me. That's what predators do. They watch people's statuses and speculate to give a word to play on their emotions. Then, boom—they can get into your bank account without you knowing they study your weaknesses. No one can blame this on me being broken; this is common sense. Then, he went on to tell me, "A real wife would have said, 'Forget it. You don't have to pay.'" "Well, I'm a fake wife, because this one is going to make you accountable—something that I notice doesn't happen often."

"Apostle, what are you teaching people? Your actions are not lining up. Operating like a bum." I had never talked down to him before, but baby, this was disgusting to me on all levels. He could compare me to whomever, but I wasn't letting anybody who looked like him mishandle me or my stuff. My laptop was so nice, and he replaced it with a Chromebook. I asked where my old laptop was. He replied, "I threw it in the garbage." This garbage ministry was killing me. I needed my stuff from the laptop. This dude was destroying my stuff like he was doing me a favor. He replaced the laptop, but he had destructive behaviors. I was supposed to be getting better, and he was allowing me to decline.

I won't allow myself to decline because of a man. I don't need love that badly. I don't need anything that badly. I was over this man and his manipulation. Girl, I wish it was done, but he continued with this selfish behavior. I refused to let this dude drain me or drag me through the mud. No way. I know my value and my worth. It just increased, and I added tax.

This was beyond me, and all he ever said was, "Are you ready for a man of God?" I was ready, but if this was what a man of God did, I was not hearing or feeling it. Weeks went by, and I was appalled at his actions. He wanted me to clean. I understand what a wife's role is. This was a huge distraction. I didn't feel like he understood. He would try to make me jealous, talking about how all these women wanted him, and I didn't care. They could have my place and position, because baby, I didn't want it at all.

I had to get my business affairs in order. He stopped supporting my live streams on social media, yet I still supported his. My husband and John stopped supporting me altogether. I was looking at them like dead flies. See, once I get a revelation on something, you can't change my mind. I was awakening each day like, My perception deceived me. I went into this thing open. I wanted to be this woman I never was before. I didn't trust anything about this predator. I noticed his subliminal messages on Facebook towards me. I was laughing like, This has to be a joke. I was still going, and he was not stopping me. I would not let it happen.

I was sleeping and heard him tell John that he looked cute. When I confronted him about it, he said John doesn't like the word "cute," so he said it. It sounded gay and appeared gay. He went out every day with this man and never asked me if I wanted to go. I wanted to know why that was. He said they were business partners, and that was what they did before me. When they would order pizza, they never asked me if I wanted any. I didn't like Pizza Hut. I am a city girl; we love New York pizza. I didn't like Pizza Hut's pizza, but that was not the only thing that was sold at Pizza Hut. I watched him do this, and I didn't complain at all. If that was normal for him, it was very abnormal for me.

If I complained about something, I was going to let them know that I saw them. The bond that they had was a relationship. John had my husband's name tattooed on his finger. I can't make any of this up. John went to McDonald's at 3:00 in the morning and got my husband something to eat. They went out and got cake—one for him and one for the other. I was so confused about what I was manipulated into. My ex-husband knew that spirit.

We were planning on going to Vegas, and God said, "I will show you things in Vegas." I was saying I needed a witness, so I called my prophet friend and told him what God had said. He told me, "Okay, let's see what God is up to." I had a conversation with my husband and told him that John had to pay rent. These dudes were cooking together and laughing. It was so disturbing to me. This was so sick. I can't make this up. During our conversation, my husband became upset with me. He said he would talk to his momma and help him find a place. He said he knew this would happen.

I paid him to do everything for me. He had to pull his weight. Why couldn't we split everything down the middle and have it be fair? My husband was telling me that he paid for Wi-Fi monthly and trash collection quarterly. I told him, "Those are not bills. Let's be fair on all things." He told me that John had just asked to pay for water and he told him no. I thought, Sir, do you know all the bills that I carry? Why wouldn't you talk to me before making this decision? That's what selfish people do. When it comes to me, I'm never considered unless you want me to preach for you for free. I am over this marriage. It was a joke to him, but I wasn't laughing. I took these vows seriously.

Let me tell you how manipulation works. I sat them down when I returned from New Jersey and told them how I felt. I wanted to work together as a team. We were all in agreement. John started ignoring all my messages. My husband could convince him to do whatever he desired. He would tell John to do my flyers. My husband had a hold on this dude. I wasn't mad; he had a hold on me in the beginning, too, so I understood. One thing I understood is that both of them were for one another. That's what lovers do. They literally did everything together, and yet again, I was married and alone.

When they weren't together, he was in John's room doing jewelry or something. My husband was in love. I remember his ex saying that he would treat me right until a boy came around.

CHAPTER 14

The church's anniversary was coming up. The people wanted to know what Prince wanted for his anniversary, and I said an Apple laptop. We decided that together, we would give him $250.00 together so he could get his laptop or whatever he desired. His best friend—or boyfriend—decided that he would go into the group chat that we created and tell the members of the church that he didn't want that. He changes his mind like the weather. We had already come to an agreement about what was going to happen for the apostle. He came back with his inappropriate self, acting like the wife in our marriage.

I was so annoyed, and I wanted to know if anyone else felt this way. I wouldn't dare call the people to alert them. I knew how my husband felt about his ministry. Anything that tried to destroy his ministry—he was not having it. A pastor called me from the ministry and said that such-and-such was out of order. I agreed and said that I would talk to Prince. I went to talk to my husband, and immediately, the situation was flipped on me. John asked, "Why do we have to get him something that he asked you for?" Immediately, my head started hurting. My husband agreed with him and said I shouldn't have told the church what he wanted. He would never ask the church to buy him something like that. The church was there to fund him. I was done on all levels.

It didn't matter what he got with the money. He was getting the money, so it didn't matter. He told me to never do this again. The pastor asked why John was so adamant about the church giving Prince money. It was so disturbing because this lady had no idea what I was facing in my house. I was wrong—again—but only when it came down to his best friend. I couldn't win, and I wasn't going to try. This marriage came with too much. The responsibility wasn't hard, but him choosing me was hard. If anyone thought that I was going to tolerate him having a boyfriend and a wife, they were crazy.

I was navigating the harsh reality that no one wanted to deal with my son. He was my focus, and I was trying to weigh my options. I would have to pull Madison out of school immediately. The drawing board was leaning towards leaving Tennessee sooner than expected. I didn't want to look strange on social media, but I didn't want to look strange to those who looked up to me, either. I won't advise anyone to deal with the spirit of perversion. I don't care who they are—you be true to God and yourself. I went into this thing clear-minded and level headed, but a collision happened along the way.

I'm not blaming him because a spirit had gotten him. That spirit was no longer going to seduce me into thinking I was nuts. I deal with my child daily by myself. I deal with a lot when it comes down to Maddy. I can't be distracted from my purpose. I was not getting my work done properly because everything was about packing his jewelry. "Do this for me and I will pay you." I had to tell him no. "Preach on this day," he would tell me, and I had no time to focus on the importance of my business. I made it my business to launch things I was supposed to drop because I didn't have his best friend to help me. I would pay someone to take his place. I was not playing about me.

Manipulation is so real. Before we went to Vegas, my husband was giving me gifts. John was giving me gifts as well, trying to throw me off of what I felt. Once upon a time, I was a manipulator, so I know the game. John brought us matching robes. He wanted to put our initials on the robes. He also bought me a selfie stick. They were trying it out after going shopping without me. "We are all going," they said, but no one invited me. I refused to ask if I could go outside with my husband. You have to let people choose for themselves, and he always chose his best friend.

We were about to have a revival, and I was so excited. My husband was coming on my platform to preach. We were still doing ministry together, and it seemed like that was all we did together. I mean, we played games a couple of times. We went on a few dates, but I have nothing to brag about. It was so simple. I love elegance and effort.

I was having my revival, and my husband was up to speak. He taught the word, and it was good, but I could notice a difference in him. My brother preached the next day and followed behind my husband's teaching.

My husband is competitive; he wanted to know what I thought. I always told him it's not good to compare. I told him what I felt. The next day, he was up on the last day. During our live streams, we take things seriously in our house. We were live on social media and Madison was making noise. I heard the washing machine starting, and I was livid because everyone stays still during my live streams. His best friend was walking back and forth. Madison was cutting all the way up. His best friend came back and put on some worldly music, and I sat back and watched the sabotage. I was so disappointed in the lack of effort.

In a couple more days, we were going to Vegas. I promised to take my husband out for our anniversary. I wanted it to be just me and him, with me eating and him recording me. I like cute stuff, but I love intimacy without a crowd. I told him I was treating him, but he had to drive. He agreed that this was what would take place. He then asked what John was going to drive and how he was going to get around. We were at the restaurant, and he was being so mean to the waitress. He was being difficult like he did with me—he wanted this, he didn't want that.

I can honestly say that when it was just me and him, he was fun. He was comical and he had a cool personality. It seemed as though we were married longer. I was so into getting my son with me full-time. He was a handful, and I wanted to make sure I was taking the proper precautions for his safety. My husband and I had a conversation about getting my son to Tennessee. My husband didn't want that to happen. He went from "Okay" to "No. Turn him over to the state." He said he didn't want to deal with it. According to him, my son would come and throw off the ministry, and it would restrict him from flowing in God.

I couldn't find out, to save my life, how I was the pastor, he was the apostle, and we couldn't cast these demons out. We had to be two powerless beings. I can't help others and neglect my baby. I believe this was the reason I couldn't get my son a ride to Tennessee. All roads led me back to New Jersey. My husband wanted to deal with grown people, but not my son. He kept saying I never told him my son was adopted. That would have changed everything concerning me and him. I told him I was a foster mom, and he said that was okay. I don't deny my children. He is my son, and I've always called him that.

My husband and I were not beefing, but I felt crazy, and I couldn't call myself a leader while turning my back on my baby. If anyone knows how to respond to him, it's me. I was not about to bury my son over a man. I know he was out of control, but he is my responsibility.

We were on our way to Vegas. It looked good. I overpacked, and we had everything we needed. I didn't mind paying $200.00 extra for the trip because I know my child. She gets dirty and she pees a lot, and she can't hold it. Either way, I was going to prepare accordingly. When we travel, my daughter gets first-class treatment on planes. We always board the plane first because of her handicap. We don't wait in line; we go right through TSA. Everyone was happy with the convenience of my baby going to Vegas. Prior to us heading to Vegas, he cooked and packed my food and made the bed. He fed Madison and had her up; all I had to do was bathe her. My husband knew that I always travel with my food. I don't eat airport food.

We got to Vegas and caught a taxi. It was beautiful, and I had my eyes alert. Again, God said something would happen in Vegas. The party began. I took my baby outside, and she loves to party. She was so amused by the lights and the live entertainment. We got dressed and walked to the Strip, where the hotel was located. The Strip was a mix of new Vegas and old Vegas. Either way, I was happy to be outside. I asked Prince where he was so Maddy and I could meet him. We met up after showering and freshening up.

We chilled, and I was concerned about Madison enjoying herself. She loves music, and I wanted to make sure she had a good time. My teenager danced the night away. I was so happy to see the joy on her face. I had taken my baby away from everyone she loved, never considering what that would do to her. My husband had split from his best friend, and he went to find him. We walked so much, but Maddy didn't even pay it any mind. She just walked without hesitation. She loved the performances.

There's all type of crazy behavior in Vegas. People be on some demon time, seriously. I witnessed that if you want to live wildly, Vegas is the place to be. It's a no-judgment zone. I understood why my husband loved this place. There were swingers, homosexuals, all types of people who were looking for a good time. I can adapt to any environment. I didn't want to bring Maddy, but Prince insisted. It was Vegas. I had been there already, so it was no big deal for me. My husband said he would rather her be with us—great way to distract me. I was okay with having her with me. We went back to the hotel because it was bedtime. I wanted to relax because my teenager had energy I didn't have. We would be there for six days, so we had five more days to have fun.

My husband and John were still out. My husband doesn't move often because of something he has with his bones. Walking often is not something that he does, but he loved the Vegas life. I was happy to be in Vegas. Everyone was happy, and I was on vacation with my husband. I envisioned us playing in the pool, holding hands, and smiling together as a family. Shut your mouth, Tanesha. I didn't spend quality time with him at all. We were Dutch on vacation—he went his way and I went mine—and it was disturbing. My daughter and I were partying alone. I would call him, and he would be chilling with his best friend. I'd never been on vacation with my spouse, and here I was, all by myself with Maddy. I paid for food and other things for myself and my daughter. He often said, "I want someone to take care of me. I can take care of myself, but you have a part to play."

My husband spoke a good game to the people of God, and it had him looking grand. Privately, he sucked at being a provider and a protector. A husband is a priest, a provider, and a protector. My husband asked the people to sow a seed on my behalf. He wanted the people to honor me. Tears fell from my eyes because I was carrying a lot financially. I could handle it, but it was a lot to take care of my children and two households. My husband told the saints that his dinner was always late because I prayed for people, when really, it was late because he was always very indecisive. One minute, he would want chicken, then turkey tails the next minute, then beans, then nothing.

He commissioned them to sow $100.00 on my behalf. I saw the people saying that they would sow. It was no big deal to me. It was the principle for me. It felt like he felt me in the spirit. That money could have helped with a bill in New Jersey. That was no big deal for me because you will reap what you sow. Prior to coming to Vegas, he didn't give me the seed that was sown into me. He had manipulated the people by using my name and lying. It wasn't strange to me because he likes people to serve and preach for free. Although I wasn't preaching, he had just lied to God's people. This was not biblical at all. Meanwhile, he didn't do anything for free. My spiritual gifts were awakened. Disclaimer: I'm no perfect individual. I simply don't have people do anything for me for free. God was about to show himself!

CHAPTER 15

I was happy to know that the Lord was about to show me something. That made me nervous, though, because I knew some kind of exposure would take place. We all stayed in the same room. Maddy and I were in bed. My husband was on the couch. His best friend was on a pull-out bed. I needed to see a close interaction between these two dudes. I needed to see gestures from them. Prior to us leaving our house and going to Vegas, my husband was dancing and sticking his tongue out while both of them were in the living room. He was looking in the kitchen to see if I noticed. I did notice, but I didn't say anything. This was so crazy to me. The less I said, the better. I wanted them to think I was blind and asleep to this affair, relationship, whatever it was. These men were bold. Some days, I thought, T, you are nuts. This is really not true! This is all in your head. Some days, I wished I was dreaming. I am from Jersey City, and I was trained to watch my surroundings. I'm alert when it appears as if I'm not paying attention.

I could be pinched now and alerted that I was dreaming. These two were in the kitchen together, cooking and laughing like husband and wife. My husband would be so happy interacting with him. His best friend knew everything about him, and he even told me some stuff. When my husband would get off live streams, John had tea waiting for him. I can't make this up. He didn't need me. I can't lie, and I won't: Their relationship was amazing. My husband can get anyone to do what he pleases. Before my awakening, I would often tell him,

"Anything you want, husband." He is charming, and he has a way of making others smile.

Manipulation is real, and not for nothing—he was a really good manipulator. I was so cheesy when we first met. Baby, that was for television. I needed someone to say, "Cut! Let's reshoot." Out of all the women in the world, I don't know why he picked me for this foolishness. I don't believe in my heart it was in vain. I believed there was a purpose in this exposure. My heart is broken for all the women who have endured the position of being a first lady with an undercover man. It's not sexy or right by far. It's disgusting to even play with someone's time or children. He is a predator who preys on women. He preys on the emotions of women. Everything he does is geared toward women—he said out of his own mouth, "You can tell a woman anything and she will believe it." He sells jewelry and does pageants, and his ministry is for women.

So, while in Vegas, he was himself. He was doing him, and I was chilling with my kid. It was so bad that dudes kept following me because I was alone. Maddy and I dined and enjoyed ourselves. We attended concerts and had a ball. Who goes on vacation and doesn't enjoy themselves? I was making the best of it. I met some bomb people, and I was excited. We all were in the room, and my husband called John a little boy. There's a story that Prince had allegedly tried to come on to a young boy years ago. It made the newspaper, and the victim said that's what Prince calls people who he likes. I'd never heard him say that before. He was into John, and he couldn't hide it at all. They left the room and got their faces painted. I asked why he didn't tell me. He said it wasn't like that.

They always did things together, leaving me out of the equation. That was not appropriate.

My husband wanted a husband and a wife. I couldn't compete. I wasn't going to, either. Run, sis, because it's not in your imagination. We got in the cab to head to the airport. My husband paid the fare. When we arrived, I was checking in with all this stuff I had, struggling in the line. My husband walked away and went to TSA without me. Run, sis! Yes, he left me. I was waiting on Maddy's wheelchair so we could all go to TSA. We had to freshen up because my daughter was wet. I used the restroom and she was having cramps. I was sweating from being left alone to handle all of this. The transporter was outside the door. I was telling her to take me so I could meet my husband; he was calling me and I was ignoring him. I had two big bags with no help, and the transporter was asking me where my husband was.

We travel together and stay together—or so I thought. Nope. He went with John and left me. I was crying and saying that if I was pregnant, he would have stayed. We approached where he was. He was sitting down next to John. I was wondering, What in the world? I wanted to curse him out so badly. I sat far from them. I told him he was a selfish bastard again. "Why would you leave me?" He said he had an important phone call. "What is so important that you would let me struggle?" "I didn't know that you were struggling." "I guess you didn't care." He will always be selfish. He came over to me and said I was not going to continue to talk down to him.

I said, "You are selfish and I won't compete." He asked, "What do you mean, 'compete'?" I ignored him and he said he was sorry. I knew he was sorry and inconsiderate as heck. I could not wrap my mind around him just leaving me in the airport. He said his selfish behavior was something that we could work on. We're cut from two different cloths. Selfish people only care about themselves. Selfish people have a one-track mind that leads back to themselves. Whew, chile, I can't make this up. I was his wife, and he really left me.

It didn't bother me because once he showed me that I was single, I believed I was single. I operated as if I was alone. I got the groceries bags out of the car. I cleaned my car out. I pumped my own gas. I dated myself daily. I went to the park alone. I did everything but sleep alone. So, this roommate that I was operating as would be no longer. I would act accordingly.

No, I never cheated. I will wear my ring until our divorce is final. He is still my husband publicly. He was throwing shots at me, trying to provoke me. I refused to allow him to make me make a post about him. I am bold. He changed his relationship status, which previously stated that he was married. He deleted our pictures together. To me, he was acting like a woman. I am quiet. He is loud. This is the same man who is allegedly supernatural; the one who walks in the spirit world daily. I was not about to act like a wife with a half-husband while in our house. It would be different if he didn't know better, but he is an apostle. He studies the word of God, and I was supposed to submit to him as he has submitted to Christ. Once he crossed the line, I had no obligation to submit to him.

John cooked for him. I stopped serving him. I stopped asking what he wanted for dinner. I stopped making him my priority. When he ordered food, I was never his priority. I wasn't foolish. I stopped cleaning as well. He said I half-cleaned, anyway. I had a conversation with him to tell him that I had to get my son. No one was fit to handle him, and no one wanted to. I asked him if I was an asset or a liability. He said I was an asset. Whew, chile, I wasn't gaining. I lost a lot of money dealing with him. If it was ever about money, I never would have married him. I love him, not the idea of him, because he isn't my type.

One day, I looked through his paperwork and noticed that John's name was on the church accounts. I was asking him questions and telling him that John had to pay rent. I wanted to see his response. It wasn't the fact that he was over the church finances. They were in love, and it became more noticeable to me. I often asked questions to see how much he was willing to do for me. He was upset and said that John was only there because of him. I then asked him why he didn't tell me who he went to Vegas with the last time. John told me freely that he went with the man his ex-wife accused him of messing with. I asked him three times on different occasions. I even asked in front of John, just for him to lie three times. He said, "Tanesha, if you think I am gay, you should just leave me alone." He kept lying, acting as if I was dumb.
I often looked dumbfounded when God was speaking to me. I won't ignore the Holy Spirit. When I was a teenager, my best friends were always gay men. He said, "Tanesha, you just want to bring up my past." Apostle, if dealing with a man was in your past, you should have never brought a guy into our home. The flesh is weak, but the spirit is willing. The devil knows how to tempt us leaders. The devil knows how to entice us leaders. The flesh couldn't handle that, and if I believed or had a clue, he wouldn't

have come into our home.

Everyone was saying they were lovers. I ignored it because I believed in this man of God. His words repeated in my head: "Are you ready for a real man of God?" Baby, everything in me was ready. Marriage is a lot, and I didn't take my vows as a joke. I was intentional about him, my feelings, and what we were about to build together. John used to try to throw me off when I first moved in, saying his family was crazy to think he was sleeping with an apostle. The crazy part about it all was that I'd seen it with my four eyes—including my contacts. Anytime John needed anything, he was at my husband's aid.

This was so uncomfortable for me. Every store run or outing they went on, they brought back cake for themselves. None for me and my baby. Some days, my husband would ask if I needed something. I needed to have that kind of service all the time. I may sound like a brat, but baby, I am royalty. I would have not needed anything back. It's the principle. I told him that every time I left the house, I thought of him. I needed this to be reciprocated. Something was wrong with this picture. Cake is not my thing, but the thought of asking me if I wanted any was my point.

I remembered the 4:00 a.m. store runs and John making sure he had what he needed. I had no place, and I was not fighting or arguing for one. Apostle was a man who openly said he doesn't have problems. Homosexuality is a battle, and deliverance only come when you desire it. You have to want freedom. I have things that God is delivering me from as I write this book. The truth is, you have to be open and honest. Every time I asked him about something concerning John, everything in him became distorted.

CHAPTER 16

A wife can target and hit some areas in prayer for her spouse. We could have touched and agreed to dismantle the spirit in him. He didn't want to pray with me. He said if I found the scripture, he would pray. A family that prays together stays together. Everyone has a past, and who am I to judge his seat? He has to give an account of what he did to me. Every time he came back home with his BFF, he acted more feminine. He denied what his ex-wife said. He denied what his BFF's grandmother said. If homosexuality was his past and his past only, why would he allow himself to be tempted?

I watched every move he made. I sat back and replayed everything after Vegas. He told me at the airport that he was not here to carry my baggage. I was silent for days, and he didn't say a word. I was manipulated, and he conquered. He didn't win the victory because I was silent and sober for days. Who was I to come into this apostle's life with a special needs child who has accidents on herself? Who was I to impose my hectic life on him? I was a woman who wanted him to be true. You couldn't convince me that this story would end so soon after it started, in the honeymoon stage. I knew that I walked into greatness.

I want to say this was a mistake, but it wasn't. I believe that purpose will come out of this. I believe that I had to embark on this. Some women and men are afraid to leave their spouses because of their titles and out of fear of others judging. If the first lady has to endure these trials, you can keep your titles. I had to seek God in a different way. I don't hate him, and I pray that deliverance will come to him. When deliverance comes, he will be all right.

I couldn't wrestle and act as if nothing was happening. I was hurt watching my husband be in love with a man. We didn't have arguments. I calmly asked if he was taking our kitchen table, and he asked what I was trying to say. Meanwhile, I was watching him pack up his stuff and not saying anything. I sped up the process and went to U-Haul to rent a truck sooner. I said I was moving out and he told me it was premeditated. He said that I am ready to leave after any little thing. The truth is, I married him for better or worse, but I will not let anyone destroy me. That spirit has the ability to destroy a woman's confidence, self-esteem, and worth.

I tried to have a conversation with him, and I told him he was in love with his BFF. I never said a name at all. John came out of the room yelling, saying he has a name. I wanted to slap him so badly. I told him I was talking to my husband. My husband told him, "Don't worry, bro. It's okay." I was talking to him using my hands, and I guess that triggered him. I apologized, and he started walking around the house as if I was trying to hit him. He went on our deck, trying to get away from me. I can't make this up. I was as calm as ever as I was speaking. John came out of the room again and said, "I told you I didn't want your man, and he said he didn't want me." He didn't say, "I am not into men." He didn't say, "That is not my life." He said, "I don't want your man." So, in my head, I was thinking, You want a man.

As time passed, John's pants were getting tighter and tighter. I recall a time when my husband called him "bae" and said that's what they say in Tennessee. I can't believe I didn't think more of that. When I tried to talk to my husband, he told me that I am gay and I like women. Whew, chile. I was so lost because I am personally not interested in women. He screamed he had proof. He makes a scene when he is mad.

Then, he said I neglect my daughter and that he had proof of that as well. I play a lot of games, but not that one. What man watches a woman neglect her child and doesn't say anything? If I neglect her, he is as guilty as me for being a leader and not stopping me from neglecting Maddy. He told me that I was lazy and didn't want to clean. I don't mind cleaning. I believed that he wanted a house nigga, one who cleans every second. I am not that, and I will never be that.

If I am rushing after I drop my baby off at school, I will go to the gym and then come back to clean. He made half the bed the entire time we were together. I confronted him, and he said we had two different blankets. I went out and brought a comforter, and he still made half the bed—his side, of course. Days were going by, and I was so uncomfortable in this house with these two dudes. I started covering up my furniture. I started really packing and taking stuff down. I stayed out during the days I had left there so I didn't have to be around them. I took my baby out to eat after school so she could have a meal. Then, we stayed at the park until bedtime. I asked him if we could be adults and split the bills for the following month. He said he didn't know. I asked him if he was going to be out of the place by the first of the month. I was trying to see when to cut the lights off. He wanted to play. I know he was having service. Truth be told, I didn't care where he went. I was trying to communicate. He gave me a dumb answer, so I emailed the company and told them to cut the lights off the next day. He had already manipulated and deceived me. I was still being godly to him. I wanted to bust everything in the house. I bowed out gracefully.

I went to get the U-Haul truck to start packing my stuff. I was packing like a man, throwing everything in the U-Haul truck. I had to go before I was on the First 48 television show. When someone is in love, there's no telling what they will do. He told me that I married him to make money. He said that's what I told him. I made money before him. He told me he married the wrong woman. I was okay with him saying that. He thought I was controllable. If he was looking for a puppet, he married the wrong one. Once I know that God is speaking to me, I know my intuition is accurate. I stand up for what's right, regardless of how anyone feels. No apostle or man is going to downgrade me or deceive me.

They tell you to cover your spouse, and I did publicly, but I refused to be his Barbie doll, plus-sized model, or pageant cover story. I know how it feels to be broken and torn down. This story should teach women to perform background checks. Honestly, there's no way of knowing who a person is unless you try. I prayed to God. God didn't stop me, and I am a seer. I stepped out on faith. I put my fears down and took a chance. If I was not anchored in God, this situation would have caused me to turn my back on my faith.

To see an apostle do all these things was

unbelievable. It was unbelievable to hear the way he spoke about his ex-wife. To be honest, he talked about her often. I didn't understand him or the way his brain functioned. I stood, and I wasn't moved. I was shaken because it was too soon for us to be like this in our marriage. I was shaken because I have fragile areas. Apostle said he wouldn't hurt me. He told me to allow him to be my antidote. No one can be your antidote. Either I can be a bitter woman or a better one from this. I was so determined to get my money back that I was about to steal his baseball cards. They were worth a lot of money, and I could get my money back by selling them. The Holy Spirit arrested me in the spirit and said, "No. I can give you more and better. Don't allow anyone to call you a thief."

Although he is circulating lies about me, I stand for truth. No matter what life may bring, I have to do what I know to be right. I'm far from perfect, but baby, I am worth it. He manipulates people, but I will do what God said: edify leaders! He can lie, but I tell the truth. I don't want people to be remorseful for me. I survived seven months. I couldn't survive seven years.

Get yourself together and make your exit. Develop a plan and execute it. We are not anyone's cover-up. Men can try to deceive you. My husband asked me, if he is gay, why is God using him? Gifts and calling come without repentance. Therefore, all people are anointed. This is not my life. Whew, chile. If I was as crazy as I once was, this situation would have been a bloodbath. I am saved this time around because I didn't yell or swing. Fighting used to be my solution.

I can't say that I caught him in any act. That spirit

115

in him was bold, and I recognized it. You can never fight a spirit in the flesh. No matter how much you pray, it has to want to come out. The day I left, I was on the highway, and I never received a phone call from him. An apostle, a man of God, would have checked on his wife no matter what. I drove for 16 hours with my baby. At the end of any argument or disagreement, we are legally bound together until the divorce is final.

We are living in times when even the very elect are deceived. Hearts are waxed cold. Can I tell you that my husband didn't love me? I believed that he loved me, but he couldn't have both. He couldn't have me and a man. He chose the asset, and that was his best friend, John. He has bank accounts in John's name, which I would never have. John does Prince's graphics and controls his live streams on social media. Me getting eliminated was the best option because I can't try to fit in.

This situation made me see that I can do all things. This came to let me see the beast inside of me. This came to encourage women that this treatment is not of God. Titles and church services mean nothing. What are you hiding that you have to cover with so many services? Are you trying to escape from your reality? We were having so many services that Spirit wasn't as visible. My husband put in for the divorce, so if you are reading this book, I am free. You can tell your story as well. We wear too many hats to be living in bondage. Yolks have to be destroyed, and they are destroyed when we as women take action. I don't care if you were married 12 times. You are not a failure. Each marriage produces something different.

As a result of this this marriage:
1. I'm more confident.
2. I understand my power.
3. I'm a threat in the kingdom.
4. I'm not exempt from trouble.
5. I can do the impossible.
6. I can make it anywhere.
7. I need my children.
8. I am really saved.
9. I have self-control.
10. Weak people hate me.
11. I'm wiser.
12. I am really peculiar.

The moral of the story is that I can continue on and on. I need you to write what your marriage has taught you. Then, take those tools and move on.

I am for marriages; healthy ones are great. I am just happy that I can identify what an unhealthy relationship looks like.

Signs to look out for in a manipulating leader:
People imposing their ideas on you
Controlling
Small lies
Always begging for money
Clever
Cunning
Deceptive behavior
Always wanting their way
Expecting handouts
Gifted
Appear as if things are perfect

Listen: The Holy Spirit is a teacher and a guide. I am led to tell this story because I am not ashamed. It

could have been worse. I could have been blind, but my eyes are open, and my spirit is different. I've learned so much from him, and I am so grateful. I won't give anyone a false imagination as if the pain is not still within me. I am in a purifying space when God is detoxing my spirit. It has gotten easier as the days go by. I have stopped crying, and I told God that if I had to free my sisters, I was willing. It affected me along the way, but not to the point that I couldn't get up and fight for leaders or myself.

I'm unsure what I am about to embark on next, but this journey had better be ready for me because I am ready for it. I just want God. I want God to take me to the nations. I want to serve like never before. I am working on my company and myself. I am working on my eating habits. I am working on the queen in me.

At this point, I have learned that selfishness is okay when you are being selfish with yourself because you are costly, and so is the oil that you carry.

I have all my babies with me, and I end this chapter refreshed...

Made in the USA
Coppell, TX
07 July 2023

18863521R00066